The Rockwool Foundation Research Unit

Crime and Partnerships

Michael Svarer

University Press of Southern Denmark

Odense 2008

Crime and Partnerships
Study No. 19

Published by:
© The Rockwool Foundation Research Unit and
University Press of Southern Denmark

Address:
The Rockwool Foundation Research Unit
Sejroegade 11
DK-2100 Copenhagen

Telephone   +45 39 17 38 32
Fax   +45 39 20 52 19
E-mail   forskningsenheden@rff.dk
Home page   www.rff.dk

ISBN 978-87-90199-11-1
ISSN 0908-3979
June 2008
Print run: 400
Printed by Special-Trykkeriet Viborg a-s

Price: 80.00 DKK, including 25% VAT

Foreword

The Board of the Rockwool Foundation decided a few years ago that their Research Unit should pursue the interest that the Foundation has in social and labour market conditions through analyses of the situation of criminals in relation to the labour market, and more broadly of aspects of the life conditions of criminals in general, both before and after their conviction.

The main focuses of the analyses in the project are the significance of conditions of life for the tendency of individuals towards criminality, and the consequences of the punishment that society imposes on criminals. Society punishes criminals in two ways: directly through the sanctions imposed for specific breaches of the law, and indirectly through the restrictions imposed on the opportunities open to criminals after their punishment, both on the labour market and in their private lives. In the present publication, Michael Svarer analyses the indirect punishment that arises from the effects of criminal conviction on the private lives of individuals. To be more precise, he analyses the effects of a criminal conviction on an individual's future chances of finding and remaining with a spouse or partner.

A book containing all the analyses from the project is being published simultaneously with this study paper by the Danish publisher Gyldendal. It is entitled *Forbryderen og samfundet. Livsvilkår og uformel Straf* (The offender and society. Life conditions and indirect punishment), and is written by Torben Tranæs and Lars Pico Geerdsen. Michael Svarer contributed analyses related to the theme of "Crime and Partnerships" to the book, and the research results that provided the material for these analyses are presented in this paper.

On behalf of the Research Unit and the author, I would like to offer my thanks to all who have contributed to the project: Duy Thanh Huynh and Peter Fallesen, for making the data available; Ulla Nørskov Nielsen for her very competent research assistance; seminar participants at Tilburg University and the Centre for Applied Microeconometrics, Copenhagen; and in particular Anna Piil Damm, Susumu Imai, Lars Pico Geerdsen and Rune Vejlin for their very useful comments. Special thanks are also due to Birgitte Højklint for reading the manuscript.

As always with the Research Unit's projects, this research has been carried out in complete academic independence and free from the influence of any party, including the Rockwool Foundation itself, who provided the necessary resources for the project.

The research group and I would like to extend our warmest thanks to the staff of the Foundation, including the Director, Elin Schmidt, and the Board, chaired by Tom Kähler, for their unfailing and generous support and cooperation.

Copenhagen, May 2008   *Torben Tranæs*

Contents

Abstract 7

1. Introduction 9

2. The association between crime and marriage market outcomes ... 11

3. Data 13

3.1 Criminal activity in Denmark – some numbers 13
3.2 Data for partnership formation analysis 14
3.2.1. Explanatory variables 16
3.3 Data for partnership dissolution analysis 18

4. Emprical strategy 20

4.1 Timing-of-events method 20
4.2 Parametrization 22
4.2.1. Extension for partnership formation analysis 23

5. Results 24

5.1 Partnership formation analysis 24
5.2 Partnership dissolution analysis 26
5.3 Discussion and sensitivity analysis 28

6. Concluding remarks 30

7. References 31

8. Appendix - tables 34

Publications in English from the Rockwool Foundation Research Unit ... 37

The Rockwool Foundation Research Unit on the Internet 40

Abstract

This paper tests whether being convicted of a crime affects marriage market outcomes. While it is relatively well documented that crime hurts in terms of reduced future income, there has been little systematic analysis on the association between crime and marriage market outcomes. This paper exploits a detailed Danish register-based data set to fill this gap in the literature. The main findings are that male convicts do not face lower transition rates into partnerships as such, but they face a lower chance of forming partnerships with females from more well-off families. In addition males who are convicted face a significantly higher dissolution risk than their law abiding counterparts.

Keywords: Crime, Marriage, Divorce.
Classification-JEL: J12

> There's a lot of strange men in cell block ten
> But the strangest of them all
> Was a friend of mine who spent his time staring at the wall
> Staring at the wall
>
> In his hand was a note that his gal had wrote
> And it proves that crime don't pay
> She was the very same gal that he robbed and stole for
> For naming her wedding day
> For naming her wedding day.
>
> *Johnny Cash - the Wall*

1. Introduction

The economic consequences of crime in terms of reduced employment possibilities and lower market wages have been shown to be quite substantial (see e.g. Waldfogel (1994), Freeman (1999), Western et al. (2001), and Holzer (2007) for the effects of incarceration and Grogger (1995) for similar albeit smaller effects for arrestees). A less investigated, but perhaps equally important, consequence of engaging in criminal activities is the potential spill-over to marriage market outcomes. The purpose of the present paper is to take a closer look at this issue.

There are numerous payoffs to forming and maintaining a partnership, and some of these returns are economic by nature. As listed in e.g. Weiss (1997) gains from marriage include specialization gains, the possibility of sharing public goods, of coordinating investment activities, and of sharing risk. To enjoy these benefits, a necessary condition is that there is someone who is willing to marry you. This paper investigates whether the possible stigma effect of being convicted for a criminal offence affects an individual's chances in the marriage market.

This paper uses a sample of Danish males (since males by far are the most active in terms of committing crime) to investigate whether being convicted of a crime affects marriage market outcomes like finding a partner, quality of partner, and dissolution risk. An obvious empirical challenge is to identify the causal effect of conviction on marriage market outcomes. It is likely that individual characteristics, both observable in the data and unobservable, affect the process related to crime and to marriage markets outcomes at the same time. To address the potential endogeneity of crime, I follow a strategy that has been used in (e.g.) the – somewhat related – literature that assesses the effects on the exit rate from unemployment of sanctioning unemployed individuals that do not comply with eligibility criteria for unemployment insurance (van den Berg et al. (2004), Abbring et al. (2005), Lalive et al. (2005), and Svarer (2007)). The method simultaneously estimates the process that describes criminal activity and the process of marriage market activities. Under some well-defined assumptions (which I will return to later), the model causally identifies the effect of crime on the transition rate into and out of partnerships (Abbring & van den Berg, 2003). Another empirical cause of concern is the possibility of reverse causality. Difficulties in finding a partner or maintaining a relationship might affect the propensity to commit crime and hence to get convicted. To address this issue, I supplement the timing-of-event methodology with an instrumental variable approach basically using pre marriage market criminal activity as instrument for being convicted in the analysis of partnership formation and pre relationship criminal activity as instrument for being convicted in the partnership dissolution analysis.

The interdependency between marriage market status and crime has been studied intensively in the sociological literature. However, the main emphasis has been on the effect of marriage on the propensity to commit crime. The conclusion from this literature is that marriage causally reduces crime (see Sampson et al. (2006)). Studies that look at the other side of the coin – the effect of crime on marriage market outcomes – are much fewer in number.

Sampson & Laub (1993) look at the relationship between juvenile delinquency and adult outcomes using US data. They find that delinquency when young is associated with weaker attachment to a spouse and higher divorce propensity in adult years. Levitt & Lochner (2001), also based on US data, find no difference in marriage or divorce patterns by age 30 for youth criminals compared to non-criminals. Lopoo & Western (2005) investigate the effect of incarceration on the formation and stability of marital unions, and using US data they find that the probability of finding a partner or divorcing the current partner is higher during incarceration, but not significantly so afterwards. Neither of these studies address the issue of endogeneity, and in that sense this paper is the first (as far as the author is aware) that investigates the causal effect of crime on marriage market outcomes.

The study uses a large Danish register-based data set to investigate how the incident of being convicted of a criminal offence affects the probability to form partnerships, the quality of partners, and the partnership dissolution risk. The data is unique in the sense that detailed information on the timing of events is accurately registered. For all criminal offences that are solved, the data contain the date of conviction. Information about criminal activities is merged to a 10% sample of the Danish population between 15 and 66 years old. The latter sample includes information on partnership start and dissolution and various socioeconomic variables for all individuals, their partners, and the parents of both individuals in a given couple. The sample is observed from 1990-2003.

The main findings are that being convicted does not affect the transition rate into partnerships as such, but males who have been convicted face a lower chance of forming partnerships with females from more well-off families, suggesting that crime does carry a penalty in terms of forming partnerships. In relation to partnership dissolution, it is found that males who are being convicted face a significantly higher dissolution risk than their law abiding counterparts.

The structure of the paper proceeds as follows. In Section 2, I first discuss what to expect in terms of the association between crime and marriage market outcome. Section 3 presents the data and the sample selections for the subsequent analysis are thoroughly described. Section 4 describes the empirical strategy and in particular under what assumptions causality inference is obtained. In Section 5 the results are presented, and finally in Section 6 I conclude.

2. The association between crime and marriage market outcomes[1]

In the classical Becker (1968) framework, individuals commit crime when the expected gain from doing so exceeds the expected cost of punishment. The marriage market literature finds that males' attractiveness is positively associated with income and labour market attachment (see e.g. Gautier et al. (2005) and Svarer (2007)), which suggests that one possible reason for committing crime is to increase individual income and thereby becoming more attractive as romantic partner. It has, however, been shown that there exists a real cost of being caught and subsequently punished for a crime related to subsequent labour market success (see e.g. Kling (2006)), it is not obvious whether this is also the case when it comes to the marriage market. It follows, however, naturally that males who have been convicted might face lower chances of attracting a partner and perhaps especially a high quality partner. Likewise, males who are found guilty of a felony and who are already in a partnership, face the risk that their partners reassess the value of the partnership and realise that it has decreased and leave the partnership. The empirical divorce literature almost consistently finds that males who experience a major drop in income have increased dissolution risks (e.g. Weiss & Willis (1997) and Svarer (2005)). On the other hand, income prospects might not be the only trait that females evaluate when they decide on who to admire romantically.

Turning an eye to the sociological literature and in particular drawing on social learning theory, it might be the case that delinquency and risk-taking behaviour in general might be seen as evidence of qualities such as nerve and bravery, which, as pointed out in Rebellon & Manasse (2004) might attract potential romantic partners. In a similar line of argumentation, Darwin's theory of sexual selection suggests that risk-taking behaviour signals high status and as a consequence increases sexual access, not only among nonhuman primates, but also among Homo sapiens. Based on data from the National Survey of Youths collected in the 1970s in the US, Rebellon & Manasse (2004) test whether delinquency is associated with the amount of romantic involvement. Having access to a panel data set with two waves, they test whether individuals who are criminal in the first wave have more romantic activity in the second wave compared to their law abiding counterparts when they condition on various personal characteristics and romantic activity in wave 1. The findings suggest that males with more delinquencies have more romantic activity in wave 2. This leads them to conclude that bad boys do get the girls. This finding is supported by e.g. Palmer & Tilley (1995), who conclude that a non-negligible reason for joining gangs in the US is to have increased sexual access to females. Although, being a criminal type might increase the chances of short term romantic encounters it does not follow that it also increases the chances of finding a long-term partner. The latter event is the focus of the current investigation.

---

1. I focus entirely on male criminality in this paper. Hence the following only view the gains and costs from delinquency from the male perspective.

Additional support for the association between crime and sexual involvement is granted by Kanazawa & Still (2000). Here it is argued that the age-crime curve (see next Section) in an evolutionary psychological theory perspective can be explained by the observation that "..intense intrasexual competition for mates among young men has produced a psychological mechanism which compels them to commit interpersonal violent crimes and property crimes in their attempt to gain reproductive access to women.." Kanazawa & Still (2000, p. 444).

Recently, Edlund et al. (2007) argue that there exists a non-random association between the skewed sex ratio for the 16-25 years old in China, as a result of the one-child policy, and the development in the crime rate, which has almost doubled from 1992-2004. According to Edlund et al. (2007) the increased competition among males for female attention has caused an increase in criminal behaviour.

In sum, criminal men might be able to raise more income to support a family by conducting crime. The act of being caught, however, signals that their future income potential is reduced, and consequently they are less attractive as marriage partners viewed from an economic perspective. However, evolutionary theory suggests that traits (mostly unobservable in data sets) which are positively correlated with criminal activities might also be positively correlated with attractiveness in the marriage market. Hence, the expected effect of convictions on partnership formation is ambiguous. The literature that has found that criminal men have more romantic involvement does not offer information on who they are romantically involved with. It could be the case that different women put different weight on the different attributes of criminals. Building on the large literature on assortative mating that finds that for most traits (like age, education, income, IQ, social status) a positive pattern emerges (see e.g. Epstein & Guttman (1984)), it could be conjectured that females from families with higher social status are likely to put more weight on the provider potential in males, and hence they would be more likely to punish criminal activity. Whether this is the case will be determined in the subsequent empirical analysis.

For couples, the situation is somewhat different. Here the risk-taking male has attracted the female, and now he has to provide for her and the family. As observed in the literature (e.g. Sambson et al. (2006)), males reduce their level of criminal activity once they are in a relationship, which might suggest that the gains to crime have diminished. Males who get convicted and who might spend some time in prison could lose their attractiveness as partners, and it is expected that the dissolution risk increases.

The remainder of the paper contributes with an empirical investigation of the association between crime and marriage market outcomes.

3. Data

The data used in this study arise from two different registers. Information on criminal activities come from the Crime Register, which is administered by the justice authorities. Information on demographic and socioeconomic characteristics of the general population comes from the integrated database for labour market research (IDA) maintained by Statistics Denmark. In the following, a 10% sample of the Danish population between 15 and 66 years old is subtracted from IDA. The sample is observed from 1990-2003. Information on criminal activities for the subsample is obtained by merging the data with the Crime Register. In the following, I refer to crime when a conviction has taken place. I know the exact date for a given conviction, the type of felony for which the conviction is given, and the sentence type. I only focus on criminal activities conducted by males. Males commit more than 80% of (solved) crimes in Denmark (source: Statistics Denmark, 2005), and since I intend to model crime behaviour, female criminal activity will be too low to give precise results. The two registers are merged by a person identifier. In Denmark all inhabitants are endowed with a personal security number. Hence, it is relatively easy to combine information from different registers since all information is registered by the personal identifier.

In the remaining part of the data section, I first give a short overview of criminal activity in Denmark. Second, I discuss sample selection and choice of explanatory variables in relation to the two sets of analyses that are carried out in this paper. I first consider how crime affects the transition rate into partnerships and the quality of partners. Subsequently, I investigate how crime affects the dissolution risk of partnerships.

3.1 Criminal activity in Denmark - some numbers

To get an impression of the amount of crime in Denmark compared to other countries, I use data from the Seventh United Nations Survey on Crime Trends and the Operations of Criminal Justice Systems[2]. The most recent US figures are from 1999 and I therefore base the comparison on 1999 numbers. Below, I report the

	Rate per 100,000 inhabitants, 1999		
	Denmark	US	England & Wales
Grand total of recorded crime	9,291.31	8,571.19	10,061.11
Total recorded intentional homicide, completed	0.98	4.55	1.45
Total recorded burglaries	1,896.90	755.29	1,721.33
Total recorded drug offences	15.60	231.29	560.11
Total recorded thefts	3,443.18	2,502.66	3,357.60

---

2. See http://www.unodc.org/unodc/en/crime_cicp_survey_seventh.html

total number of recorded crimes in the US, England & Wales and Denmark. In addition, I report some numbers by type of crime.

The figures presented above suggest that the crime rate is not lower in Denmark compared to countries like England & Wales and the US. The crime pattern varies somewhat. The US has a remarkably higher homicide rate and more drug offences than the two other countries, whereas burglaries and thefts are more pronounced in the European examples.

In Figure 1, I present the age specific crime rate for 2003. The figure shows the fraction in each age group that has been convicted of a crime in 2003.

Figure 1

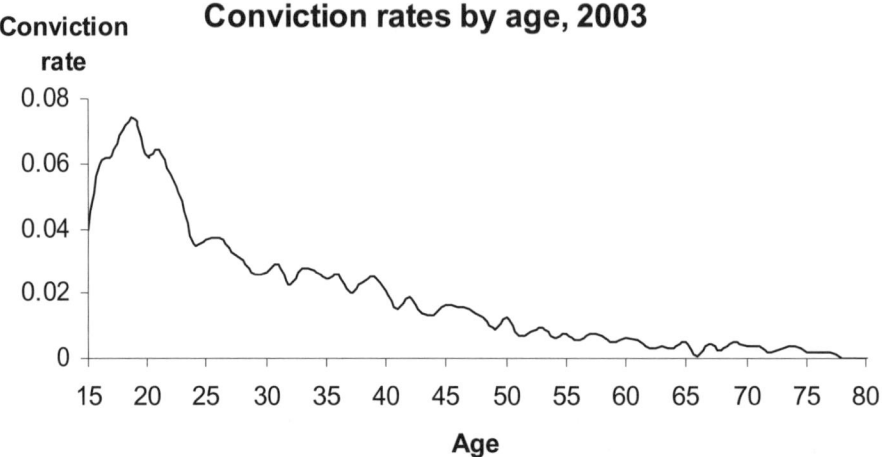

Figure 1 confirms that a non-negligible number of individuals are found guilty of criminal felonies. The age pattern suggests that the propensity to commit crime dies out when individuals grow older and peaks around the age of 18 (see e.g. Levitt & Lochner (2001) and Freeman (1999) for similar age patterns for the US). In fact, Hirschi & Gottfredson (1983) claim that this relationship is similar in all social and cultural conditions. As mentioned in the earlier section, Kanazawa & Still (2000) provided a marriage market explanation for the robustness of the shape across countries, namely that males undertake risky and criminal activities to gain access to females. In relation to the purpose of the current study, it is interesting that most crime is undertaken by individuals when they are young, which is the time when they are becoming active in the marriage market.

3.2 Data for partnership formation analysis

Data for partnership formation is collected by sampling all males as they enter the marriage market. I assume that this occurs at age 18, and I consequently flow sample all males when they turn 18. I then follow them through time until they either form a partnership or the sampling period ends. The sampling framework has the advantage that I do not have to model left censored partnership observation since the incident of partnership is non-existing before individuals turn 18.

A partnership can take the form of legal marriage or cohabitation. The latter partnership form is widely used in Denmark, and of those who marry, more than 80% premaritally cohabit (see e.g. Svarer (2004)). Since data on marriage market behaviour come from register data, I have no information on partnerships that do not entail shared housing (i.e. dating is not observed). I therefore measure the time until a male gets formally married or shares a housing unit with a female[3]. Dates of both occasions are given on a daily basis in the registers.

In the subsequent empirical analysis, I investigate whether being convicted affects the transition rate into partnership[4]. I only look at the effect of the first conviction. That is, I do not investigate the marginal effect of subsequent convictions for the same individual. This approach is similar to the literature on the effect of UI benefit payment sanctions on the exit rate from unemployment (see van den Berg et al. (2004), Abbring et al. (2005), Lalive et al. (2005), and Svarer (2007)), and has the advantage that the empirical model becomes more tractable. The strategy is, however, not completely innocuous since, as will become clear later, many males who have been convicted once get convicted again. Preferably, the empirical model should allow for multiple convictions. The econometric literature is, however, not particularly well-developed to address the endogeneity issues that arise in these situations and as a short-cut I follow the route of many predecessors and consider the first conviction (event) only. Related to the results that follow this decision might not be to detrimental to the main results of the study that compares marriage market outcomes of convicted to non-convicted. The drawbacks of the empirical model is more serious when I look at the effects of different crime types and sentences. By restricting focus to the first conviction I risk to measure the effect of the least serious crime and the mildest sentence. I will return to these issues when I interpret my results in Section 5.

To account for confounding characteristics of the individuals, I include a number of explanatory variables. In addition, I also analyse whether a criminal conviction affects the quality of the marriage partner. Unfortunately, the data do not contain information on beauty, weight, IQ or other characteristics that could be used to assess the attractiveness of females. I therefore follow the strategy in

---

3. Notice that this implies that individuals who are sharing housing without having a real partnership are registered as cohabitors. In circumstances where the age difference is larger than 15 years or the two individuals are biologically related, they are not registered as cohabitors. I have no further information to disentangle these observations from true partnerships. On the other hand, they are presumably few in number and the alternative is to ignore cohabitations. I am reluctant to follow this strategy since cohabitation is by far the most frequent partnership type, especially among the younger cohorts in Denmark.

4. I use convictions as indicators for crime. Alternatively, I could have investigated how charges and conviction affect arriage market behaviour. There are a number of arguments for focusing on convictions only. First, conviction might be more visible to the market than charges (that might be dropped) and therefore more likely to cause a change in marriage market possibilities. Second, the empirical investigation is kept more tractable when only convictions are endogenized. Anyway, results from an empirical model where both charges and convictions are modelled (a long the lines of Lalive et al. (2005)) provide the same main conclusions as the current analysis.

Gautier et al. (2005) and use income and educational measures for attractiveness. Since individuals in the sample typically match when they are quite young, and therefore before they have completed an education and entered the labour market, I use information on the fathers of the females as a proxy for quality of females[5]. I use the following information to proxy quality (all measured at the year of partnership start): a dummy for whether the wealth of the father is in the top 50% of the wealth distribution, a dummy for whether the disposable income of the father is in the top 50% of the income distribution, and a dummy for whether the father has completed a medium or long-term further education. The former two are time-varying.

I also investigate whether different types of criminal activities and sentences have different effects on partnership formation. Specifically, I look at the following crime classifications: violence, property and others (which include sexual offences and drug crimes) and the following four types of sentences: mandatory prison sentence, suspended prison sentence, fine, and community service plus other sentences[6]. I do not include traffic crimes in the analysis. Descriptive statistics for these variables are presented alongside the explanatory variables in Table 1.

3.2.1 Explanatory variables

In the subsequent analysis, the following variables are included; age, children, an indicator variable taking the value 1 if the individual has children, student, an indicator for currently attending school, work, indicator if the individual is currently working (the reference category for school or work is unemployed), gross income is the sum of personal income, capital income, housing benefit, child support, and tax free retirement subsidies and is inflated to 2003 price level using the official wage deflator published by Statistics Denmark, unemployment rate, gives the annual average unemployment rate. Wealth father, an indicator variable that equals 1 if the father of the male has a level of wealth in the top 50% of the wealth distribution, and educated father, which is an indicator variable that takes the value 1 if the father has completed a medium or long term further education. Again, the latter two variables are included to reflect the marriage quality of the male who has not yet been able to signal his earnings potential in the labour market.

All variables are time-varying and up-dated on an annual basis. The explanatory variables are included both in a model for partnership formation and in a model that estimates the time until an individual is convicted. In the latter model

---

5. Chadwick & Solon (2002) present evidence that the intergenerational transmission of income status between fathers and daughters is quite substantial.
6. In some cases more sentences are issued simultaneously. I.e. a male can get a suspended sentence and a fine. In the following I record type of sentence according to how severe they are. A mandatory prison sentence is assumed to be the toughest followed by suspended prison sentence, fines and community service plus other sentences. That is, in the example mentioned above the male will be recorded with a suspended prison sentence.

I also include an indicator variable convicted before 18 that takes the value 1 if the person has received a conviction prior to his 18th birthday and mother, which is an indicator variable that takes the value 1 if the mother has completed a medium or long term further education. Table 1 gives descriptive statistics for the data set used. In total, I observe 32170 young men from the age of 18 until they either form a partnership or the observation period ends. I disregard observations for which there are missing information on the included variables in the analysis, which primarily is due to missing information on parents characteristics.

Table 1: Descriptive statistics for partnership formation sample

Variables:	Mean	Std.dev
Criminal activities		
Conviction	0.0987	
-violent	0.0193	
-property	0.0528	
-other	0.0266	
Sentence		
Suspended sentence	0.0165	0.1275
Mandatory sentence	0.0068	0.0822
Fine	0.0435	0.2039
Other	0.0319	0.1756
Individual characteristics		
Unemployment degree (fraction of year)	0.0468	0.1387
Fraction that start partnerships	0.4912	
Mean age at partnership start	22.0877	3.0762
Gross income (in 2003 DKK)	168781	120331
Student	0.4367	
Working	0.4484	
Criminal before age 18	0.0385	
Males' characteristics		
Wealth father (in 2003 DKK)	415392	2088574
Father is highly educated	0.3083	
Number of individuals	32170	

Table 1 shows that around 10% of the males get convicted during the observation period, which again indicates that criminal activity is not a rare event among Danish youths. To supplement this around 4% of the sample were convicted before they turned 18. Most crimes are property crime followed by violent crimes. The convictions typically result in a fine or community service[7]. Very few of the young men in the sample get a mandatory prison sentence. Around 49% of the individuals form a partnership during the period and the mean age at which this happens is 22.

---

7. Note that since I only look at first conviction, the sentences tend to be milder than if I also considered repeat offenders.

3.3 Data for partnership dissolution analysis

Data for the partnership dissolution analysis is obtained by flow sampling all relationships that start in the sampling period. The main objective of this analysis is to investigate whether being convicted affects the length of a given relationship. Information on convictions are similar to the data set used in the partnership formation analysis.

The included explanatory variables are; age, for both partners, children, an indicator variable taking the value 1 if the couple has children, working, indicator for whether either of the spouses work, man older/woman older, indicator for whether the age difference is larger than 4 years (in both directions), gross income, for both individuals in the couple the sum of personal income, capital income, housing benefit, child support, and tax free retirement subsidies is included, and numbers are inflated to 2003 price level using the official wage de-

Table 2: Descriptive Statistics for partnership dissolution sample.

Variables:	Mean	Std.dev
Criminal activities		
Conviction	0.030	
-violent	0.007	
-property	0.016	
-other	0.007	
Sentence		
Suspended sentence	0.005	
Mandatory sentence	0.004	
Fine	0.010	
Other	0.011	
Individual characteristics		
Age, male	24.943	5.260
Age, female	23.570	5.514
Children	0.640	
Working, male	0.756	
Working, female	0.767	
Male older (>4 years)	0.197	
Female older (>4 years)	0.060	
Gross income, male (in 2003 DKK)	290009	222685
Gross income, female (in 2003 DKK)	197704	103862
Formally married	0.314	
Low education, male	0.389	
High education, male	0.124	
Low education, female	0.487	
High education, female	0.155	
Males' characteristics		
Unemployment rate (fraction of a year)	0.050	0.150
Wealth father (in 2003 DKK)	546245	2254364
Father is highly educated	0.192	
Convicted prior to relationship start	0.212	
Relationship information		
Mean length of partnership (in years)	3.983	3.268
Fraction of partnerships that dissolve	0.364	0.481
Number of relationships	39370	

flator published by Statistics Denmark, married, an indicator for whether the couple is formally married or cohabiting, low education, indicator for whether the highest completed educational level of either person is lower than vocational training, high education, indicator for whether the highest completed education of either person is medium- or long-term further education (the reference category consists of individuals with vocational or short-term further education), married, an indicator variable distinguishing between cohabitating and formally married couples.

In the crime equation, I include the same list of variables as in the partnership formation analysis plus an indicator variable, conviction prior to partnership start, that takes the value 1 if the event has occurred.

Descriptive statistics for the data used in the partnership dissolution analysis are presented in Table 2.

Men who have a partner commit less crime than single men. Compared to Table 1, the fraction of males who have been convicted is now around 3% measured at the moment of dissolution or when the sample period ends. Clearly, this sample is also older, which might explain most of the difference. However, as pointed out by e.g. Sampson et al. (2006), partnerships seem to protect males from committing crime. Again, most convictions are for property crimes, and the sentence is often fine or community service plus other sentences. Around 36% of the partnerships that begin in the sampling period ends in dissolution. The mean length of partnerships is around 4 years. The average length of formal marriages in Denmark is around 7 years (Svarer, 2005). The inclusion of cohabiting unions, which are typically shorter, reduces the average length of partnerships.

4. Emperical strategy

In order to investigate the effect of being convicted on the exit rate to and from partnership, I use duration models. Since the occurrence of a conviction is potentially endogenous to the partnership process, the goal is to disentangle the selection effect from the causal effect. Following Abbring and van den Berg (2003), I apply the timing-of-event model[8]. That is, I estimate the process into and out of partnership simultaneously with the process of being convicted, allowing the processes to be interdependent through the unobservable heterogeneity terms. Below, I present the finer details of the timing-of-event model. In the partnership formation analysis, I look at a competing risks specification where I distinguish between single males who join partnership with females of different qualities. Specifically, I group females into two marriage market segments depending on the characteristics of their fathers. In the partnership dissolution analysis, I look at a single risk specification. Below, I present the basic model illustrated as a situation of partnership dissolution. After this I discuss the amendments for the partnership formation analysis.

4.1 Timing-of-events method[9]

The timing-of-events method enables me to identify the causal effect of convictions on the exit rate from partnerships. The estimation strategy requires simultaneous modelling of the conviction rate and the partnership hazard. Let $T_{p(artnership)}$ and $T_{c(onviction)}$ denote the duration of a partnership and the duration until a male gets convicted. Both duration variables are continuous nonnegative random variables. I allow them to interact through correlation of unobservables and through a possible treatment effect of getting convicted on the partnership hazard. I assume that all individual differences in the joint distribution of the processes can be characterized by observed explanatory variables, x, and unobserved variables, v. The occurrence of a conviction and the exit rate out of partnerships are characterized by the moments at which they occur, and I am interested in the effect of the realization of T_c on the distribution of T_p. The distributions of the random variables are expressed in terms of their hazard rates $h_c\left(t|x_{c,t}, v_c\right)$ and $h_p\left(t|t_{convicted}, x_{p,t}, v_p\right)$. Conditional on x_p and v_p, I can therefore ascertain that the realization of T_c affects the shape of the hazard of T_p from t_c onwards in a deterministic way. This independence assumption implies that the causal effect is captured by the effect of t_c on $h_p\left(t|t_{convicted}, x_{p,t}, v_p\right)$ for $t > t_c$. This rules out that t_c $h_p\left(t|t_{convicted}, x_{p,t}, v_p\right)$ for $t \leq t_c$, i.e. anticipation of the conviction has no effect on the partnership dissolution hazard. This assumption could potentially be a bit strong in the context of convictions, since trials normally are announced some time in advance, e.g. when

---

8. Notice, that this identification strategy has been applied in a related situation where the goal is to estimate the causal effect of unemployment benefit sanctions on the exit rate from unemployment (see van den Berg et al. (2004), Abbring et al. (2005), Lalive et al. (2005), and Svarer (2007)).
9. The basic model presented in this section corresponds to the model used by Lalive et al. (2005).

the crime is detected and a charge is filed. However, the *exact* outcome of the trial is unknown, since the acused might be found not guilty or the charges might be dropped. Abbring & van den Berg (2003) show that the assumption only requires that the exact date is not known - the agents are allowed to know the distribution of the timing. Furthermore, as noted by Abbring & van den Berg (2003), the time span between the moment at which the anticipation occurs and the moment of the actual sentence is short relative to the duration of relationships. This implies that the potential bias in the effect of convictions on the relationship hazard presumably is rather small. In addition it is not obvious in the present context what kind of information that is available to the other marriage market participants. It might be natural to assume that it is easier to hide the filing of a charge than the conviction itself. Hence, the reactions to a conviction in terms of marriage market outcomes are likely to happen after the moment the conviction is given. Given the independence and no anticipation assumptions, the causal effect of a conviction on the partnership dissolution hazard rate is identified by a mixed proportional hazard model. That is, it is a product of a function of time spent in the given state (the baseline hazard), a function of observed time-varying characteristics, x_t, and a function of unobserved characteristics, v

$$h(t|x_t,v) = \lambda(t) \cdot \varphi(x_t,v),$$

where $\lambda(t)$ specified as $\exp(\lambda_m(t))$ is the baseline hazard and $\varphi(x_t,v)$ is the scaling function specified as $\exp(\beta'x_t + v)$. More specifically the system of equations is:

$$h_c(t|x_{c,t},v_c) = \exp(\beta'_c x_{c,t} + \lambda_c(t) + v_c) \qquad (1)$$

$$h_p(t|t_{conviction}, x_{p,t}, v_p) = \exp(\beta'_p x_{p,t} + \delta_1 D(t_{conviction}) + \lambda_p(t) + v_p), \qquad (2)$$

where x_c, x_p are vectors of possible time-varying covariates, $D(t_{conviction}) \equiv I(t_{conviction} < t)$ is a time-varying indicator variable and v_c and v_p are unobserved heterogeneity terms.

Intuitively, the timing-of-events method uses variation in partnership duration and in duration until a conviction (conditional on observed characteristics) to identify the unobserved heterogeneity distribution. The selection effect is captured by the correlation between v_p and v_c, while the causal effect of the conviction on partnership duration is captured by the effect of the conviction conditional on the observables and v_p and v_c.

The empirical model is non-parametrically identified without the use of instrumental variables on the basis of the mixed proportional hazard assumption (Abbring and van den Berg, 2003) and also on the basis of time-varying explanatory variables (e.g. Brinch, 2007). It is possible to strengthen identification through various sources. One is the use of repeated spells (see e.g. van den Berg, 2001). In the present context this is however not particular attractive. First, in the partnership formation analysis I focus on the time until first partnership and allowing for repeated spells requires that conditional on observable characteristics, the unobserved heterogeneity terms of an individual do not change over time (see e.g. Roed & Westlie, 2007). This is problematic if partnership formation and partnership duration are affected by duration dependence and this is not appropriately addressed in the econometric model. Given the duration of typical partnerships my data is not rich enough to allow for careful treatment of repeated spells of singlehood and partnerships. Second, in the partnership formation analysis the unobserved heterogeneity term is related to the partnership and not to the particular person. It does not seem appropriate to assume a time-invariant unobserved heterogeneity term across different partnerships for a given person.

An additional source of identification can be obtained through the use of exclusionary restrictions. That is, variables that affect the conviction rate, but not the partnership formation or dissolution rate. In the subsequent analysis, I will supplement the timing-of-event model with pre marriage market and pre partnership convitions as instruments.

4.2 Parametrization

The baseline hazards, $\lambda_p(t), \lambda_c(t)$, are specified as a piecewise constant hazard, where I divide the time line into a number of intervals. For all hazards, I divide the time line into $M = 3$ intervals measured in days (0-1200, 1200-3600, 3600-), and I let $\lambda_i(t) = (\lambda_{i1},...,\lambda_{i3})$, $i = partnership, conviction$ denote the estimated parameters in these intervals.

I use a flexible and widely applied specification of the distribution of the unobservables; it is that each unobserved heterogeneity term follows a discrete distribution with only two mass-points. One of the mass-points in each marginal distribution is normalized to zero so $V_p \in \{v_p^1 = 0, v_p^2\}$ and $V_c \in \{v_c^1 = 0, v_c^2\}$. This normalization is required as a consequence of the piecewise constant baseline specification. The correlation between V_p, and V_c is important because this is the way in which this procedure allows selection on unobservables without a resulting bias in the estimates. The associated probabilities for all the possible combinations from the discrete distributions are defined as

$$P_1 = \Pr(V_p = v_p^1, V_c = v_c^1)$$
$$P_2 = \Pr(V_p = v_p^2, V_c = v_c^1)$$
$$P_3 = \Pr(V_p = v_p^1, V_c = v_c^2)$$
$$P_4 = \Pr(V_p = v_p^2, V_c = v_c^2)$$

where $0 \leq P_j \leq 1, j = 1,2,3,4$ and $\sum_{j=1}^{4} P_j = 1$. For more details on this class of mixture distributions in duration models, see e.g. van den Berg (2001).

The parameters are found by maximizing the corresponding log-likelihood function.

4.2.1 Extension for partnership formation analysis

In the partnership formation analysis, I also distinguish between the quality of partners as measured by their fathers' wealth, income and level of education. In order to accommodate this, I specify a competing risks version of the model presented above. I include an additional random variable, $J = \{1,2\}$, which denotes the exit state from singlehood. Compared to the basic model this extension introduces an additional hazard function into partnership. The cause-specific hazard function for entry into partnerships takes the following form:

$$h_{p,j}\left(t \mid t_{conviction}, x_{p,j,t}, v_{p,j}\right) = \exp\left(\beta'_{p,j} x_{p,j,t} + \delta_{1,j} D\left(t_{conviction}\right) + \lambda_{p,j}(t) + v_{p,j}\right), \quad (3)$$

where $h_p = \sum_{j=1}^{2} h_{p,j}$. This specification introduces a new unobserved heterogeneity term, which in line with the preceding specification, is assumed to have two points of support. Hence, there are now eight possible combinations of the three unobserved heterogeneity distributions.

5. Results

In this section, I first present the results for the partnership formation analysis and then for the partnership dissolution analysis. For both analyses, I report how men who have been convicted of a crime are affected in the market for partnerships compared to men who have not been convicted. For various reasons, this comparison may be noisy. First, among those who are not convicted are potentially many criminals. In particular, these criminals might be the more talented criminals who are successful in their occupation and do not get caught and sentenced by the authorities. Second, the information about criminal behaviour might (or might not) be more visible to potential marriage partners than what is observed in the registers. I keep these complications in mind in the following.

5.1 Partnership formation analysis

As a starting point, I present in Table 3 the results from a single risk partnership formation model. That is, where I do not distinguish between the quality of the potential partner, but only consider the transition from singlehood to partnership. This analysis reveals that being convicted does not affect the exit rate from singlehood into partnerships as such. This suggests that there is no obvious marriage market penalty for convicted men in the Danish marriage market.

The other explanatory variables in the partnership hazard show that males who are older, have a higher income and are not unemployed are more likely to form partnerships. These results are in accordance with other studies on partnership formation (see e.g. Aassve et al. (2002) and Xie et al. (2003)). The unobserved heterogeneity terms (not shown) reveal a negative association between the unobserved heterogeneity terms in the partnership formation hazard and

Table 3: Results from partnership formation analysis by hazard rates, criminal activity modelled

	Partnership		Conviction	
	Coeff	Std err	Coeff	Std err
Criminal activities				
Conviction	-0.0426	0.0715		
Individual characteristics				
Unemployment degree (fraction of year)	**0.3625**	0.0822	**1.458**	0.1184
Age	**1.9722**	0.1097	**-0.9455**	0.2038
Gross income (in 2003 DKK)	**2.1769**	0.0657	-0.7433	0.3482
Student	**0.1705**	0.0421	**-0.6952**	0.0639
Working	**0.2684**	0.0415	**-0.3024**	0.0687
Criminal before age 18			**1.8943**	0.0572
Parents' characteristics				
Wealth father	**-0.1893**	0.0488	**-0.5964**	0.163
Father is highly educated	**-0.133**	0.0324	**-0.4157**	0.0647
Mother is highly educated			**-0.2387**	0.045
Number of individuals		32170		

Note: To save space, estimates for baseline hazards and unobserved heterogeneity terms are not presented
Bold figures denote significance at 5% level

in the conviction hazard[10]. That is, those who based on unobservables, are less likely to form partnerships are more likely be convicted of a crime. This pattern works, in some sense, against the intuition provided in Section 2. Here I argued that a reason why men commit crime might be to attract women – either by increasing their income and wealth or by signalling bravery and nerve. On the other hand, the males that are identified as criminal in the current analysis are those that get caught. This tentatively suggests that based on unobservable characteristics there is a group of men that are neither succesful as criminals or as marriage market participants. Supporting evidence for this interpretation can be found in Mocan & Tekin (2006). Based on US data they find that being very attractive reduces a young adult's (ages 18-26) propensity for criminal activity and being unattractive increases it for a number of crimes.

In the conviction hazard, I find that males who are younger, unemployed and who come from poorer households have higher conviction rates. These findings are in accordance with the literature that looks at determinants of crime (see e.g. Levitt & Lochner (2001) and Imai et al. (2006)). In addition, there is a remarkable high rate of recidivism. The conviction hazard for those who were already convicted prior to their 18th birth day is more than 500% higher than for those who turned 18 with a clean record.

To proceed, I present in Table 4 the results for a competing risks partnership formation analysis where I distinguish between female partners by the wealth level of their fathers[11]. The first columns give the estimates for males who match with females who have a father with wealth belonging to the top 50% of the wealth distribution (measured in the year of partnership formation). Being convicted reduces the hazard rate into partnership with women from more wealthy families with 29% (exp(-0,35)-1=-29%). In terms of forming partnerships with females from low wealth backgrounds, the incident of being convicted does not significantly affect the partnership formation rate. In sum, Tables 3 and 4 show that being convicted of a crime does not affect the rate at which young males form partnerships, but it reduces the rate at which they form partnerships with females from more successful backgrounds even after we condition on a number of other characteristics of the males.

The earlier literature on the association between crime and partnership formation (e.g. Sampson & Laub (1993), Levitt & Lochner (2001), and Lopoo & Western (2005)) did not find strong effects on being convicted on subsequent partnership formation chances. The single risk results in the current analysis corroborates these earlier findings. The results presented in Table 4 therefore highlights the relevance of distinguishing between different types of partners as the results show that being convicted is associated with a reduced partnership formation rate with women from more well-off backgrounds.

In Tables 5 and 6 (see appendix), I have investigated whether the effects of

---

10. In fact, the unobserved heterogeneity terms are perfect negatively correlated. In order to empirically identify the mass points and related probabilities I had to restrict the correlation to be either 1, -1 or 0. It turned out that -1 gave the best fit in terms of likelihood value.

11. To save space, I do not present the results for the analysis where I use level of education or income as quality proxies - the qualitative findings are similar to the results presented here.

26 Results

Table 4: Results from competing risks partnership formation analysis by hazard rates, criminal activity modelled.

Partner's father has	Partnership high wealth level		Partnership low wealth level		Conviction	
	Coeff	Std err	Coeff	Std err	Coeff	Std err
Criminal activities						
Conviction	**-0.3462**	0.0894	0.0922	0.0830		
Individual characteristics						
Unemployment degree (fraction of year)	**0.2803**	0.1209	**0.5398**	0.1348	**1.5374**	0.1178
Age	**2.6902**	0.1356	**1.8691**	0.1583	**-1.1500**	0.1993
Gross income (in 2003 DKK)	**2.8651**	0.1510	**3.2618**	0.1993	-0.5288	0.3279
Student	**0.2995**	0.0580	-0.0092	0.0640	**-0.7630**	0.0591
Working	**0.3073**	0.0581	0.1164	0.0643	**-0.3700**	0.0645
Criminal before age 18					**1.9293**	0.0528
Parents' characteristics						
Wealth father	**-0.3560**	0.0797	**-0.5284**	0.1109	**-0.2950**	0.1240
Father is highly educated	-0.0903	0.0391	**-0.2912**	0.0469	**-0.3475**	0.0601
Mother is highly educated					**-0.2765**	0.0424
Number of individuals			32170			

Note: To save space, estimates for baseline hazards and unobserved heterogeneity terms are not presented
Bold figures denote significance at 5% level

conviction on partnerships formation rates are affected by the type of committed crime and the sentence. It should be noted that the empirical model does not allow for causal interpretation of the crime or sentence specific effects since I do not model crime specific conviction rates in the current speification of the model. It is relatively easy to extend the econometric model to do this, but the low occurrence of some types of crime and sentences would lead to rather imprecise statistical estimates. Instead, I hold on to the model presented in the previous section and interpret the findings accordingly.

Relating to type of crime, I find no association between violent crime and partnership rates, whereas property and other crime are negatively correlated with the formation of partnerships with females from more well off families. In relation to type of sentence, the results, somewhat surprisingly, do not suggest a significant penalty of mandatory or suspended prison sentences. Most likely, this finding is due to the relative low incidence of these sentences in the sample. Again, these relationships are not the main focus of the current investigation and a richer data set and a more elaborate econometric model is required to make further progress in this directions. Something which is left for future work.

5.2 Partnership dissolution analysis

In Table 7, I present the results from the dissolution hazard model.

Being convicted significantly increases the dissolution risk by around 76%. There is accordingly a rather substantial marriage market penalty for being convicted of a crime. In the sense that being convicted for a crime signals reduced future income and hence provider potential the result corroborates other findings in the partnership dissolution literature that show that reduced income (e.g. Weiss & Willis (1997) and Svarer (2005)), higher levels of unemployment (e.g. Ahituv & Lerman (2005)) and increased sickness (e.g. Murray (2000)) for men

Table 7: Results for partnership dissolution analysis.

	Dissolution		Conviction	
	Coeff.	Std.dev	Coeff.	Std.dev
Criminal activities				
Conviction	**0.570**	0.077		
Children	**-0.078**	0.013		
Age, male	**-0.130**	0.035		
Age, female	-0.015	0.033		
Gross income, male	**-0.779**	0.076		
Gross income, female	-0.110	0.127		
Working, male	**-0.152**	0.021		
Working, female	**-0.144**	0.021		
Formally married	**-1.798**	0.038		
Male older	**0.206**	0.028		
Female older	**0.378**	0.042		
Low education, male	**0.188**	0.019		
High education, male	**-0.074**	0.037		
Low education, female	**0.233**	0.021		
High education, female	**-0.171**	0.037		
Formally married			-0.084	0.096
Children			**0.146**	0.046
Unemployment rate			**1.126**	0.146
Age			**-0.363**	0.077
Gross income			**-3.136**	0.266
Working			-0.144	0.079
Low education			**0.665**	0.088
High education			**-0.655**	0.259
Wealth father			-0.488	5.563
Father is highly educated			**-0.682**	0.126
Criminal before age 18			**2.772**	0.101
Number of couples		39370		

Note: To save space, estimates for baseline hazards and unobserved heterogeneity terms are not presented
Bold figures denote significance at 5% level

increase the risk of partnership dissolution. Combining this finding with the results from the previous section indicates that although entry into partnerships is not reduced by a criminal record exit is. There could be several reasonable explanations for this apparent time inconsistency. On the more anecdotal level some women might get attracted by the traits of criminal men and believe that once they are protected by the partnership their destructive behaviour stop. In many cases this might be true (see e.g. Sampson et al. (2006)), but in relationships were criminal activities continue the women might realize that the deviation between expected and realised utility of the partnership is too large to keep the value of continuation above the value of the outside options. Another explanation might be that, as the partnership formation analysis revealed, criminal men are more likely to form partnership with female from less well-off and less educated families than with females from more well-off families. These women are more likely to be low educated themselves and the increased dissolution risks might go through the formation of couples between low educated men and low educated women. Although, the partnership dissolution analysis try to capture this by including levels of education and income of both partners there might still be characteristics of the partners that are unobserved in the analysis both which are determinants of the partnership formation process and which positively affects the dissolution risk.

In terms of the unobserved heterogeneity terms I again find a negative correlation[12]. That is, those who based on unobservable characteristics are more likely to end their partnership are less likely to get convicted. Based on the findings in the partnership formation analysis this is somewhat unexpected. This implies that compared to a model where being convicted is treated as an exogenous event the effect of conviction on dissolution risk presented in Tables 7-9 increases. In models where being convicted is treated as an exogenous variable there is, however, also a positive association between conviction and dissolution risk.

The findings for the remaining (control) variables in the dissolution hazards are in close accordance with previous analyses of dissolution risks (see e.g. Svarer & Verner (2008)).

In Tables 8 and 9 (see appendix), I distinguish between different types of crimes and sentences. Again, these findings can not be given a causal interpretation conditional on the econometric model. Still, all types of crime are associated with increased dissolution risks, and whereas the same is true for type of sentences, there is – perhaps not surprisingly – a remarkable higher dissolution risk if the sentence leads to mandatory prison. In Lopoo & Western (2005) it is found that men who are incarcerated face a higher divorce risk while they are in prison, but not afterwards. The present study also suggests that incarceration is associated with a significantly higher dissolution risk, but so are other sentences too. The results shown in Table 7 that being convicted raises the dissolution hazard is therefore not driven solely by men who recieve a mandatory prison sentence.

5.3 Discussion and sensitivity analysis

In the preceding sections I have presented the results from an analysis where I have relied on empirical identification from a timing-of-event duration model that basically use a functional form assumption: the proportional hazard formulation, as main ingredient to sort between selection and causal effect of being convicted for a crime on subsequent success in the marriage market. The advantage of this identification strategy is partly that it has been applied succesfully in the literature that has evaluated how "convictions" for unemployed in terms of reductions in unemployment insurance benefits, if they do not comply eligibility criteria, have affected their exit rate from unemployment (see e.g. van den Berg et al. (2004), Abbring et al. (2005), and Lalive et al. (2005)). In addition, that the timing-of-event model has been shown to be quite robust to various misspecifications (Gaure et al. (2007)). However, as the analysis have shown I needed to impose restrictions

---

12. Again, I had to restrict the correlation to be either 1, -1 or 0 to obtain empirical identification. It turned out that -1 gave the best fit in terms of likelihood value.

on the correlation between the unobserved heterogeneity terms to obtain empirical identification, which of course questions the power of the estimates. It therefore seems appropriate to ask (1) what would the results have been if I have not addressed endogeneity of convictions, (2) are the findings sensitive to different specifications of the timing-of-event model, and (3) are there superior identification strategies that can be used given the available data.

The address the first question, I have estimated models where I disregard the conviction hazard and hence treat the conviction dummy as an exogenous indicator variable. The findings form this model are in close accordance with the results presented in Table 3, 4, and 7. That is, I find that convictions are not associated with a reduce partnership formation rate as such, but that the rate at which convicted males form partnerships with females from more well-off families is significantly reduced. In terms of dissolution risk, I also find that convicted men are more likely to experience a split-up. So although, the introduction of the conviction hazard improves the fit of the model and changes the size of the coefficient somewhat it does not alter the main conclusion. This suggest that either allowing convictions to be endogenously related to the marriage market processes is not particular important or, perhaps more likely, that the empirical model does not do a very good job in terms of determining convictions. Recently, Dills et al. (2008) summarize the last 40 years of economic literature on determinants of crime, and conclude that economists know little about the empirical relevant determinants of crime. Whether this conclusion is correct or not the current analysis could be interpreted along these lines. That is, the process that describes conviction is not very well determined which implies that caution should be taken when giving the findings in this study a causal interpretation.

Related to the second question, I have experimented with different empirical specifications based on the timing-of-event model. So far it has not changed the overall conclusions. I have in particular looked a the following variations of the presented models: (1) a model where I follow all males from age 15 and therefore do not include indicator for pre marriage market convictions, (2) like the current analysis without information on previous convictions and education of mother, (3) a model where I include information on charges. That is, first I model the time until a charge is filed and in addition I model the time from charge until (possible) conviction.

As discussed in detail in Dills et al. (2008), economists have experimented with several strategies to determine crime including arrest and incarceration rates, police levels, abortion laws etc. While all of these have attractive explanations supporting their usefullness as crime instruments they also share a common deficit in terms of predicting crime rates across time and regions. The identification strategy pursued in this article is new to the crime literature and is chosen based on features of the current data set, which is rich on conviction and marriage market dynamics, but not on exogeneous variation in conviction rates. Future research in this area might benefit from a combination of longitudinal data on crime and partnership dynamics and more suitable candidates to instrument crime.

6. Concluding remarks

This paper tests whether being convicted of a crime affects marriage market outcomes. The paper finds that criminal men do suffer in the marriage market. First, they can expect to marry females from less well-off families, and second they can expect to hold on to their spouses for a shorter period of time. It is clearly difficult to compare the costs of crime in the marriage market to the costs measured in the labour market in terms of reduced wages and lower employment. The finding of this paper, however, suggests that looking at the consequences of crime should also make room for how the marriage market is affected.

7. References

Aassve, A., S. Burgess, A. Chesher, and C. Propper (2002). "Transitions from Home to Marriage of Young Americans", *Journal of Applied Econometrics*, 17, 1-23.

Abbring, J. and G. van den Berg (2003). "The Non-Parametric Identification of Treatment Effects in Duration Models", *Econometrica*, 71, 1491-1517.

Abbring, J., G. van den Berg, and J. van Ours (2005). "The Effect of Unemployment Insurance Sanctions on the Transition Rate from Unemployment to Employment", *Economic Journal*, 115, 602-630.

Ahituv, A. and R. I. Lerman (2005). "Job Turnover, Wage Rates, and Marital Stability: How Are They Related?", *IZA Discussion Paper* 1470.

Becker, G.S. (1968). "Crime and Punishment: An Economic Approach", *Journal of Political Economy*, 76, 169-217.

Brinch, C. N. (2007). "Nonparametric Identification of the Mixed Hazards Model with Time-Varying covariates", *Econometric Theory*, Vol. 23, 349-354.

Chadwick, L. and G. Solon (2002). "Intergenerational Income Mobility among Daughters", *American Economic Review*, 92, p. 335-344.

Dills, A. K., J. A. Miron, and G. Summers (2008). "What do Economists Know About Crime", *NBER Working Paper* 13759.

Edlund, L., Li, H., Yi, J., and Zhang, J. (2007). "More Men, More Crime: Evidence from China's One-Child Policy", *IZA Discussion paper* 3214.

Epstein E. and R. Guttman (1984). "Mate Selection in Men: Evidence, Theory, and Outcome", *Social Biology*, 31, 243-78.

Freeman, R. (1999). "The Economics of Crime", *Handbook of Labor Economics*, Vol 3, 3529-3571, Elsevier Science B.V.

Gaure, S., K. Røed and T. Zhang (2007). "Time and Causality: A Monte Carlo Assessment of the Timing-of-Events Approach", *Journal of Econometrics*, 141, 1159-1195.

Gautier, P.A., M. Svarer, and C.N. Teulings (2005). "Marriage and the City", Working Paper 2005-01, Department of Economics, University of Aarhus.

Grogger, J. (1995). "The Effect of Arrests on the Employment and Earnings of Young Men", *Quarterly Journal of Economics*, 110(1), 51-71.

References

Hirschi, T. and M. Gottfredson (1983). "Age and the Explanation of Crime", *American Journal of Sociology*, 89, 552-584.

Holzer, H. (2007). "Collateral Costs: The Effects of Incarceration on the Employment and Earnings of Young Workers", *IZA Discussion Paper* 3118.

Huynh, D.T., S. Imai, and T. Tranæs (2005). "Registered Criminal Activities and Labor Market Performance; A Danish Micro-data Panel, 1980-1999", Draft Rockwool Research Unit.

Imai, S., H. Katayama, and K. Krishna (2006). "Crime and Young Men: The Role of Arrest, Criminal Experience and Heterogeneity", *NBER Working Paper* 12221.

Kanazawa, S. and M.C. Still (2000). "Why Men Commit Crimes (and Why They Desist)", *Sociological Theory*, 18(3), 434-447.

Kling, J. (2006). "Incarceration Length, Employment and Earnings", *American Economic Review*, 96:3, 863-876.

Lalive, R., J. Van Ours, and J. Zweimüller (2005). "The Effect of Benefit Sanctions on the Duration of Unemployment", *Journal of the European Economic Association*, 3(6):1-32.

Levitt, S. and L. Lochner (2001). "The Determinants of Juvenile Crime", in J. Gruber (ed.), Risky Behavior Among Youths: An Economic Analysis, University of Chicago Press: Chicago.

Lopoo, L.M. and B. Western (2005). "Incarceration and the Formation and Stability of Marital Unions", *Journal of Marriage and the Family*, 67, 721-734.

Mocan, N. and E. Tekin (2006). "Ugly Criminals", *NBER Working Paper* 12019.

Murray, J. E. (2000). "Marital Protection and Marital Selection: Evidence from a Historical-Prospective Sample of American Men", *Demography*, 37(4), 511-521.

Palmer, C.T. and C.F. Tilley (1995). "Sexual Access to Females as a Motivation for Joining Gangs: An Evolutionary Approach", *Journal of Sex Research*, 32(3), 213-217.

Rebellon, C.J. and M. Manasse (2004). "Do "Bad Boys" Really Get the Girls? Delinquency as a Cause and Consequence of Dating Behaviour Among Adolescents", *Justice Quarterly*, 21(2), 355-389.

Røed, K. and L. Weslie (2007). "Unemployment Insurance in Welfare States: Soft Constraints and Mild Sanctions", *IZA Discussion Paper* 2877.

Sampson, R.J. and J.H. Laub (1993). Crime in the Making: Pathways and Turning Points Through Life, Harvard University Press.

Sampson, R.J., J.H. Laub, and C. Wimer (2006). "Does Marriage Reduce Crime? A Counterfactual Approach to Within-Individual Causal Effects", *Criminology*, 44(3), 465-508.

Svarer, M. (2004). "Is Your Love in Vain? Another Look at Premarital Cohabitation and Divorce", *Journal of Human Resources*, 39(2), 523-536.

Svarer, M. (2005). "Two Tests of Divorce Behaviour on Danish Marriage Market Data", *Nationaløkonomisk Tidsskrift (Danish Economic Journal)*, 143(3), 416-432.

Svarer, M. (2007). "Working late: Do Workplace Sex Ratios Affect Partnership Formation and Dissolution", *Journal of Human Resources*, 42(3), 583-595.

Svarer, M. (2007). "The Effect of Sanctions on the Job Finding Rate: Evidence from Denmark", *IZA Discussion Paper* 3015.

Svarer, M. and M. Verner (2008). "Do Children Stabilize Danish Marriages?", *Journal of Population Economics*, 21, 395-417.

The Seventh United Nations Survey on Crime Trends and the Operations of Criminal Justice Systems (1998 - 2000) (http://www.unodc.org/unodc/en/crime_cicp_survey_seventh.html).

van den Berg, G. (2001). "Duration Models: Specification, Identification, and Mulitple Durations", in J.J. Heckman and E. Leamer, eds., *Handbook of Econometrics*, Vol. V, North Holland, Amsterdam.

van den Berg, G., B. van der Klaauw and J. van Ours (2004). " Punitive Sanctions and the Transition Rate from Welfare to Work" , *Journal of Labor Economics*, 22, 211-241.

Waldfogel, J. (1994). "The Effect of Criminal Conviction on Income and The Trust "Reposed in Workmen"", *Journal of Human Resources*, 29(1), 62-81.

Weiss, Y. (1997). "The Formation and Dissolution of Families: Why Marry? Who Marries Whom? And What Happens Upon Divorce", *Handbook of Population and Family Economics*, Elsevier Science B.V.

Western, B., J. Kling and D. Weiman (2001). "The Labour Market Consequences of Incarceration", *Crime and Delinquency*, 47(3), 410-427.

Xie, Y, J.R. Raymo, K. Goyette, and A. Thornton (2003). "Economic Potential and Entry into Marriage and Cohabitation", *Demography*, 40(2), 351-367.

8. Appendix

Table 5: Results from competing risks partnership formation analysis by hazard rates, criminal activity modelled.

Partner's father has	Partnership high wealth level		Partnership low wealth level		Conviction	
	Coeff	Std err	Coeff	Std err	Coeff	Std err
Criminal activities						
Violence	-0.1120	0.1259	0.1316	0.1078		
Property	**-0.3623**	0.0828	-0.0040	0.0741		
Other	**-0.5180**	0.1288	0.0153	0.1038		
Individual characteristics						
Unemployment degree (fraction of year)	**0.2932**	0.1157	**0.4952**	0.1086	**1.4521**	0.1189
Age	**1.5076**	0.1106	**1.1492**	0.1093	**-0.8684**	0.2017
Gross income (in 2003 DKK)	**2.6508**	0.1910	**2.8051**	0.1960	**-0.7028**	0.3484
Student	**0.3991**	0.0605	0.0895	0.0550	**-0.6893**	0.0639
Working	**0.3644**	0.0610	**0.1932**	0.0554	**-0.2952**	0.0689
Criminal before age 18					**1.9001**	0.0573
Parents' characteristics						
Wealth father	**-0.1761**	0.0847	**-0.2527**	0.0588	**-0.6336**	0.1489
Father is highly educated	-0.0289	0.0388	**-0.1481**	0.0391	**-0.4196**	0.0647
Mother is highly educated					**-0.2354**	0.0450
Number of individuals			32170			

Note: To save space, estimates for baseline hazards and unobserved heterogeneity terms are not presented
Bold figures denote significance at 5% level

Table 6: Results from competing risks partnership formation analysis by hazard rates, criminal activity modelled.

Partner's father has	Partnership high wealth level		Partnership low wealth level		Conviction	
	Coeff	Std err	Coeff	Std err	Coeff	Std err
Sentence						
Suspended sentence	-0.1741	0.1416	-0.0889	0.1288		
Mandatory sentence	0.1592	0.2023	0.2604	0.1924		
Fine	**-0.3970**	0.0976	0.0506	0.0852		
Other	**-0.3962**	0.1321	0.0878	0.1044		
Individual characteristics						
Unemployment degree (fraction of year)	**0.2651**	0.1159	**0.5009**	0.1085	**1.4370**	0.1188
Age	**1.5854**	0.1122	**1.2065**	0.1097	**-1.1212**	0.2020
Gross income (in 2003 DKK)	**2.6440**	0.1911	**2.6876**	0.1937	-0.5796	0.3481
Student	**0.3842**	0.0605	0.0888	0.0550	**-0.7178**	0.0640
Working	**0.3503**	0.0611	**0.2025**	0.0554	**-0.3227**	0.0690
Criminal before age 18					**1.8901**	0.0574
Parents' characteristics						
Wealth father	**-0.2242**	0.0838	**-0.2249**	0.0586	**-0.6098**	0.1568
Father is highly educated	-0.0270	0.0390	**-0.1512**	0.0392	**-0.4302**	0.0648
Mother is highly educated					**-0.2309**	0.0451
Number of individuals			32170			

Note: To save space, estimates for baseline hazards and unobserved heterogeneity terms are not presented
Bold figures denote significance at 5% level

Table 8: Results for partnership dissolution analysis.

	Dissolution		Conviction	
	Coeff.	Std.dev	Coeff.	Std.dev
Criminal activities				
Violence	**0.540**	0.082		
Property	**0.486**	0.060		
Other	**0.603**	0.078		
Children	**-0.080**	0.013		
Age, male	**-0.141**	0.035		
Age, female	-0.006	0.033		
Gross income, male	**-0.752**	0.076		
Gross income, female	-0.102	0.127		
Working, male	**-0.152**	0.021		
Working, female	**-0.139**	0.021		
Formally married	**-1.797**	0.038		
Male older	**0.208**	0.028		
Female older	**0.361**	0.042		
Low education, male	**0.186**	0.019		
High education, male	-0.071	0.037		
Low education, female	**0.234**	0.021		
High education, female	**-0.170**	0.037		
Formally married			-0.042	0.096
Children			**0.145**	0.046
Unemployment rate			**1.188**	0.145
Age			**-0.413**	0.077
Gross income			**-3.212**	0.253
Working			-0.124	0.079
Low education			**0.646**	0.087
High education			**-0.690**	0.260
Wealth father			-0.417	5.514
Father is highly educated			**-0.661**	0.127
Criminal before age 18			**2.770**	0.101
Number of couples		39370		

Note: To save space, estimates for baseline hazards and unobserved heterogeneity terms are not presented
Bold figures denote significance at 5% level

Table 9: Results for partnership dissolution analysis.

	Dissolution		Conviction	
	Coeff.	Std.dev	Coeff.	Std.dev
Sentence				
Suspended sentence	**0.555**	0.118		
Mandatory sentence	**0.913**	0.126		
Fine	**0.475**	0.101		
Other	**0.527**	0.097		
Children	**-0.078**	0.013		
Age, male	**-0.128**	0.035		
Age, female	-0.016	0.033		
Gross income, male	**-0.780**	0.076		
Gross income, female	-0.115	0.127		
Working, male	**-0.151**	0.021		
Working, female	**-0.143**	0.021		
Formally married	**-1.799**	0.038		
Male older	**0.206**	0.028		
Female older	**0.380**	0.042		
Low education, male	**0.188**	0.019		
High education, male	**-0.073**	0.037		
Low education, female	**0.233**	0.021		
High education, female	**-0.171**	0.037		
Formally married			-0.036	0.096
Children			**0.153**	0.046
Unemployment rate			**1.216**	0.146
Age			**-0.414**	0.077
Gross income			**-3.255**	0.249
Working			-0.131	0.079
Low education			**0.646**	0.088
High education			**-0.691**	0.260
Wealth father			-0.399	5.531
Father is highly educated			**-0.678**	0.127
Criminal before age 18			**2.774**	0.101
Number of couples		39370		

Note: To save space, estimates for baseline hazards and unobserved heterogeneity terms are not presented
Bold figures denote significance at 5% level

Publications in English from the Rockwool Foundation Research Unit

Time and Consumption
Edited by Gunnar Viby Mogensen. With contributions by Søren Brodersen, Thomas Gelting, Niels Buus Kristensen, Eszter Körmendi, Lisbeth Pedersen, Benedicte Madsen. Niels Ploug, Erik Ib Schmidt, Rewal Schmidt Sørensen, and Gunnar Viby Mogensen (Statistics Denmark, Copenhagen. 1990)

Danes and Their Politicians
By Gunnar Viby Mogensen (Aarhus University Press. 1993)

Solidarity or Egoism?
By Douglas A. Hibbs (Aarhus University Press. 1993)

Welfare and Work Incentives. A North European Perspective
Edited by A.B. Atkinson and Gunnar Viby Mogensen. With Contributions by A.B. Atkinson, Richard Blundell, Björn Gustafsson, Anders Klevmarken, Peder J. Pedersen, and Klaus Zimmermann (Oxford University Press. 1993)

Unemployment and Flexibility on the Danish Labour Market
By Gunnar Viby Mogensen (Statistics Denmark, Copenhagen. 1994)

On the Measurement of a Welfare Indicator for Denmark 1970-1990
By Peter Rørmose Jensen and Elisabeth Møllgaard (Statistics Denmark, Copenhagen. 1995)

The Shadow Economy in Denmark 1994. Measurement and Results
By Gunnar Viby Mogensen, Hans Kurt Kvist, Eszter Körmendi, and Søren Pedersen (Statistics Denmark, Copenhagen. 1995)

Work Incentives in the Danish Welfare State: New Empirical Evidence
Edited by Gunnar Viby Mogensen. With contributions by Søren Brodersen, Lisbeth Pedersen, Peder J. Pedersen, Søren Pedersen, and Nina Smith (Aarhus University Press. 1995)

Actual and Potential Recipients of Welfare Benefits with a Focus on Housing Benefits, 1987-1992
By Hans Hansen and Marie Louise Hultin (Statistics Denmark, Copenhagen. 1997)

The Shadow Economy in Western Europe. Measurement and Results for Selected Countries
By Søren Pedersen. With contributions by Esben Dalgaard and Gunnar Viby Mogensen (Statistics Denmark, Copenhagen. 1998)

Immigration to Denmark. International and National Perspectives
By David Coleman and Eskil Wadensjö. With contributions by Bent Jensen and Søren Pedersen (Aarhus University Press. 1999)

Nature as a Political Issue in the Classical Industrial Society: The Environmental Debate in the Danish Press from the 1870s to the 1970s
By Bent Jensen (Statistics Denmark, Copenhagen. 2000)

Foreigners in the Danish newspaper debate from the 1870s to the 1990s
By Bent Jensen (Statistics Denmark, Copenhagen. 2001)

The integration of non-Western immigrants in a Scandinavian labour market: The Danish experience
By Marie Louise Schultz-Nielsen. With contributions by Olaf Ingerslev, Claus Larsen, Gunnar Viby Mogensen, Niels-Kenneth Nielsen, Søren Pedersen, and Eskil Wadensjö (Statistics Denmark, Copenhagen. 2001)

Immigration and the public sector in Denmark
By Eskil Wadensjö and Helena Orrje (Aarhus University Press. 2002)

Social security in Denmark and Germany – with a focus on access conditions for refugees and immigrants. A comparative study
By Hans Hansen, Helle Cwarzko Jensen, Claus Larsen, and Niels-Kenneth Nielsen (Statistics Denmark, Copenhagen. 2002)

The Shadow Economy in Germany, Great Britain, and Scandinavia. A measurement based on questionnaire surveys
By Søren Pedersen (Statistics Denmark, Copenhagen. 2003)

Do-it-yourself work in North-Western Europe. Maintenance and improvement of homes
By Søren Brodersen (Statistics Denmark, Copenhagen. 2003)

Migrants, Work, and the Welfare State
Edited by Torben Tranæs and Klaus F. Zimmermann. With contributions by Thomas Bauer, Amelie Constant, Horst Entorf, Christer Gerdes, Claus Larsen, Poul Chr. Matthiessen, Niels-Kenneth Nielsen, Marie Louise Schultz-Nielsen, and Eskil Wadensjö (University Press of Southern Denmark. 2004)

Black Activities in Germany in 2001 and in 2004. A Comparison Based on Survey Data
By Lars P. Feld and Claus Larsen (Statistics Denmark, Copenhagen. 2005)

From Asylum Seeker to Refugee to Family Reunification. Welfare Payments in These Situations in Various Western Countries
By Hans Hansen (Statistics Denmark, Copenhagen. 2006)

A Comparison of Welfare Payments to Asylum Seekers, Refugees, and Reunified Families. In Selected European Countries and in Canada
By Torben Tranæs, Bent Jensen, and Mark Gervasini Nielsen (Statistics Denmark, Copenhagen. 2006)

Employment Effects of Reducing Welfare to Refugees
By Duy T. Huynh, Marie Louise Schultz-Nielsen and Torben Tranæs (The Rockwool Foundation Research Unit. 2007)

Determination of Net Transfers for Immigrants in Germany
By Christer Gerdes (The Rockwool Foundation Research Unit. 2007)

What happens to the Employment of Native Co-Workers when Immigrants are Hired?
By Nikolaj Malchow-Møller, Jakob Roland Munch, and Jan Rose Skaksen (The Rockwool Foundation Research Unit. 2007)

Immigrants at the Workplace and the Wages of Native Workers
By Nikolaj Malchow-Møller, Jakob Roland Munch, and Jan Rose Skaksen (The Rockwool Foundation Research Unit. 2007)

Crime and Partnerships
By Michael Svarer (The Rockwool Foundation Research Unit. 2008)

The Rockwool Foundation Research Unit on the Internet

Completely updated information, e.g. about the latest projects of the Research Unit, can always be found on the Internet under the home page of the Research Unit at the address: www.rff.dk

The home page includes in a Danish and an English version:

- a commented survey of publications stating distributors of the books of the Reseach Unit
- survey of research projects
- information about the organization and staff of the Research Unit
- information about data base and choice of method and
- newsletters from the Research Unit

Printed newsletters free of charge from the Rockwool Foundation Research Unit can also be ordered on telephone +45 39 17 38 32.